My Encounter with God Before Sunrise

A MEDITATION & PRAYER JOURNAL
FOR WOMEN OF FAITH

This journal is a gentle space for you to slow down, seek God and rest in His presence.

Each day follows the rhythm of R.E.S.T. a sacred guide to draw you closer to the heart of God.

R- Receive the Word: Open your Bible and your heart. Let His truth speak to you.
E- Examine Its Truth: Pause and reflect. What is God revealing today?
S- Surrender and Soak: Linger in stillness. Let the Word settle deep.
T- Talk to the Father: Write your prayers. Be open, honest, anf expectant.

Let this journal become your morning altar where peace begins and God meets you.

BIBLICAL MEDITATION

"Be still, and know that I am God."
-Psalm 46:10

Biblical meditation is the practice of slowing down and focusing your heart on God's presence and His Word. It is not about emptying your mind- *but filling your soul with truth.*

1. *Find Stillness*
- Choose a quie place. Sit comfortably. Allowing yourself to breathe deeply. Close your eyes or lower gaze.

2. *Breathe with Intention*
- Inhale: *Lord, I receive Your Breath...*
- Exhale: *My life is shaped by Your will...*

3. *Focus on Scripture*
- Read your choosen verse or passage slowly.

4. *Reflect & Listen*
- What is God revealing to me right now?
- How does this verse speak to my life today.
- Sit in silence.

5. *Respond in Prayer or Journaling*
- Write your thoughts and prayers down.

Reminder: There's no perfect way to meditate. The goal is simply to meet with God. To rest in His presence, receive His peace, and to be reminded of who you are in Him.

R.E.S.T

A Reflective Path For Spiritual Growth

Date:_____
S M T W T F S

RECEIVE THE WORD

Write out the scripture.

_____

_____

_____

_____

_____

EXAMINE IT'S TRUTH

What is the scripture saying to you?

_____

_____

_____

_____

_____

SURRENDER

How can you apply this to your life?

_____

_____

_____

_____

_____

TALK TO THE FATHER

Ask God to help apply the verse.

_____

_____

_____

_____

MEDITATION

Turn on soft music and close your eyes for 3-5 minutes

Inhale: Lord you breathe in me
Exhale: I am formed by your design

What can you do today to strengthen your walk with Christ

One word to describe your mood

One thing that I am grateful for today

Prayer Request

R.E.S.T

Date:_____

S M T W T F S

A Reflective Path For Spiritual Growth

R ECEIVE THE WORD

Write out the scripture.

_____
_____
_____
_____
_____

E XAMINE IT'S TRUTH

What is the scripture saying to you?

_____
_____
_____
_____

S URRENDER

How can you apply this to your life?

_____
_____
_____
_____

T ALK TO THE FATHER

Ask God to help apply the verse.

_____
_____
_____
_____

MEDITATION

Turn on soft music and close your eyes for 3-5 minutes

Inhale: Lord you breathe in me
Exhale: I am formed by your design

What can you do today to strengthen your walk with Christ

One word to describe your mood

One thing that I am grateful for today

Prayer Request

R.E.S.T
A Reflective Path For Spiritual Growth

Date:_____
S M T W T F S

Receive The Word

Write out the scripture.

_____

_____

_____

_____

Examine It's Truth

What is the scripture saying to you?

_____

_____

_____

_____

Surrender

How can you apply this to your life?

_____

_____

_____

_____

Talk To The Father

Ask God to help apply the verse.

_____

_____

_____

_____

MEDITATION

Turn on soft music and close your eyes for 3-5 minutes

Inhale: Lord you breathe in me
Exhale: I am formed by your design

What can you do today to strengthen your walk with Christ

One word to describe your mood

One thing that I am grateful for today

Prayer Request

R.E.S.T

A Reflective Path For Spiritual Growth

Receive The Word

Write out the scripture.

_____
_____
_____
_____
_____

Examine It's Truth

What is the scripture saying to you?

_____
_____
_____
_____

Surrender

How can you apply this to your life?

_____
_____
_____
_____

Talk To The Father

Ask God to help apply the verse.

_____
_____
_____
_____

MEDITATION

Turn on soft music and close your eyes for 3-5 minutes

Inhale: Lord you breathe in me
Exhale: I am formed by your design

What can you do today to strengthen your walk with Christ

One word to describe your mood

One thing that I am grateful for today

Prayer Request

R.E.S.T
Date:_____
S M T W T F S

A Reflective Path For Spiritual Growth

RECEIVE THE WORD

Write out the scripture.

_____

_____

_____

_____

_____

EXAMINE IT'S TRUTH

What is the scripture saying to you?

_____

_____

_____

_____

SURRENDER

How can you apply this to your life?

_____

_____

_____

_____

TALK TO THE FATHER

Ask God to help apply the verse.

_____

_____

_____

_____

MEDITATION

Turn on soft music and close your eyes for 3-5 minutes

Inhale: Lord you breathe in me
Exhale: I am formed by your design

What can you do today to strengthen your walk with Christ

One word to describe your mood

One thing that I am grateful for today

Prayer Request

R.E.S.T
A Reflective Path For Spiritual Growth

Date:_____
S M T W T F S

Receive The Word

Write out the scripture.

_____

_____

_____

_____

_____

Examine It's Truth

What is the scripture saying to you?

_____

_____

_____

_____

_____

Surrender

How can you apply this to your life?

_____

_____

_____

_____

Talk To The Father

Ask God to help apply the verse.

_____

_____

_____

_____

_____

Meditation

Turn on soft music and close your eyes for 3-5 minutes

Inhale: Lord you breathe in me
Exhale: I am formed by your design

What can you do today to strengthen your walk with Christ

One word to describe your mood

One thing that I am grateful for today

Prayer Request

R.E.S.T

A Reflective Path For Spiritual Growth

Date:_____

S M T W T F S

Receive The Word

Write out the scripture.

_____

_____

_____

_____

_____

Examine It's Truth

What is the scripture saying to you?

_____

_____

_____

_____

Surrender

How can you apply this to your life?

_____

_____

_____

_____

Talk To The Father

Ask God to help apply the verse.

_____

_____

_____

_____

MEDITATION

Turn on soft music and close your eyes for 3-5 minutes

Inhale: Lord you breathe in me
Exhale: I am formed by your design

What can you do today to strengthen your walk with Christ

One word to describe your mood

One thing that I am grateful for today

Prayer Request

R.E.S.T

A Reflective Path For Spiritual Growth

Date:_____
S M T W T F S

Receive The Word

Write out the scripture.

_____
_____
_____
_____
_____

Examine It's Truth

What is the scripture saying to you?

_____
_____
_____
_____

Surrender

How can you apply this to your life?

_____
_____
_____
_____

Talk To The Father

Ask God to help apply the verse.

_____
_____
_____
_____

MEDITATION

Turn on soft music and close your eyes for 3-5 minutes

Inhale: Lord you breathe in me
Exhale: I am formed by your design

What can you do today to strengthen your walk with Christ

One word to describe your mood

One thing that I am grateful for today

Prayer Request

R.E.S.T

A Reflective Path For Spiritual Growth

Receive The Word

Write out the scripture.

_____
_____
_____
_____
_____

Examine It's Truth

What is the scripture saying to you?

_____
_____
_____
_____
_____

Surrender

How can you apply this to your life?

_____
_____
_____
_____
_____

Talk To The Father

Ask God to help apply the verse.

_____
_____
_____
_____
_____

MEDITATION

Turn on soft music and close your eyes for 3-5 minutes

Inhale: Lord you breathe in me
Exhale: I am formed by your design

What can you do today to strengthen your walk with Christ

One word to describe your mood

One thing that I am grateful for today

Prayer Request

R.E.S.T

A Reflective Path For Spiritual Growth

Receive The Word

Write out the scripture.

_____

_____

_____

_____

_____

Examine It's Truth

What is the scripture saying to you?

_____

_____

_____

_____

Surrender

How can you apply this to your life?

_____

_____

_____

_____

Talk To The Father

Ask God to help apply the verse.

_____

_____

_____

_____

MEDITATION

Turn on soft music and close your eyes for 3-5 minutes

Inhale: Lord you breathe in me
Exhale: I am formed by your design

What can you do today to strengthen your walk with Christ

One word to describe your mood

One thing that I am grateful for today

Prayer Request

R.E.S.T

A Reflective Path For Spiritual Growth

Receive The Word

Write out the scripture.

_____

_____

_____

_____

_____

Examine It's Truth

What is the scripture saying to you?

_____

_____

_____

_____

_____

Surrender

How can you apply this to your life?

_____

_____

_____

_____

_____

Talk To The Father

Ask God to help apply the verse.

_____

_____

_____

_____

_____

MEDITATION

Turn on soft music and close your eyes for 3-5 minutes

Inhale: Lord you breathe in me
Exhale: I am formed by your design

What can you do today to strengthen your walk with Christ

One word to describe your mood

One thing that I am grateful for today

Prayer Request

R.E.S.T

A Reflective Path For Spiritual Growth

Receive The Word

Write out the scripture.

_____

_____

_____

_____

_____

Examine It's Truth

What is the scripture saying to you?

_____

_____

_____

_____

_____

Surrender

How can you apply this to your life?

_____

_____

_____

_____

_____

Talk To The Father

Ask God to help apply the verse.

_____

_____

_____

_____

_____

Meditation

Turn on soft music and close your eyes for 3-5 minutes

Inhale: Lord you breathe in me
Exhale: I am formed by your design

What can you do today to strengthen your walk with Christ

One word to describe your mood

One thing that I am grateful for today

Prayer Request

R.E.S.T

A Reflective Path For Spiritual Growth

Receive The Word

Write out the scripture.

_____

_____

_____

_____

_____

Examine It's Truth

What is the scripture saying to you?

_____

_____

_____

_____

Surrender

How can you apply this to your life?

_____

_____

_____

_____

Talk To The Father

Ask God to help apply the verse.

_____

_____

_____

_____

Meditation

Turn on soft music and close your eyes for 3-5 minutes

Inhale: Lord you breathe in me
Exhale: I am formed by your design

What can you do today to strengthen your walk with Christ

One word to describe your mood

One thing that I am grateful for today

Prayer Request

R.E.S.T

A Reflective Path For Spiritual Growth

RECEIVE THE WORD

Write out the scripture.

_____
_____
_____
_____
_____

EXAMINE IT'S TRUTH

What is the scripture saying to you?

_____
_____
_____
_____
_____

SURRENDER

How can you apply this to your life?

_____
_____
_____
_____
_____

TALK TO THE FATHER

Ask God to help apply the verse.

_____
_____
_____
_____
_____

MEDITATION

Turn on soft music and close your eyes for 3-5 minutes

Inhale: Lord you breathe in me
Exhale: I am formed by your design

What can you do today to strengthen your walk with Christ

One word to describe your mood

One thing that I am grateful for today

Prayer Request

R.E.S.T
A Reflective Path For Spiritual Growth

Date:_____
S M T W T F S

Receive The Word

Write out the scripture.

_____

_____

_____

_____

_____

Examine It's Truth

What is the scripture saying to you?

_____

_____

_____

_____

_____

Surrender

How can you apply this to your life?

_____

_____

_____

_____

_____

Talk To The Father

Ask God to help apply the verse.

_____

_____

_____

_____

_____

Meditation

Turn on soft music and close your eyes for 3-5 minutes

Inhale: Lord you breathe in me
Exhale: I am formed by your design

What can you do today to strengthen your walk with Christ

One word to describe your mood

One thing that I am grateful for today

Prayer Request

R.E.S.T
A Reflective Path For Spiritual Growth

RECEIVE THE WORD

Write out the scripture.

_____

_____

_____

_____

_____

EXAMINE IT'S TRUTH

What is the scripture saying to you?

_____

_____

_____

_____

SURRENDER

How can you apply this to your life?

_____

_____

_____

_____

TALK TO THE FATHER

Ask God to help apply the verse.

_____

_____

_____

_____

MEDITATION

Turn on soft music and close your eyes for 3-5 minutes

Inhale: Lord you breathe in me
Exhale: I am formed by your design

What can you do today to strengthen your walk with Christ

One word to describe your mood

One thing that I am grateful for today

Prayer Request

R.E.S.T

A Reflective Path For Spiritual Growth

Date:_____

S M T W T F S

Receive The Word

Write out the scripture.

_____
_____
_____
_____
_____

Examine It's Truth

What is the scripture saying to you?

_____
_____
_____
_____
_____

Surrender

How can you apply this to your life?

_____
_____
_____
_____
_____

Talk To The Father

Ask God to help apply the verse.

_____
_____
_____
_____
_____

MEDITATION

Turn on soft music and close your eyes for 3-5 minutes

Inhale: Lord you breathe in me
Exhale: I am formed by your design

What can you do today to strengthen your walk with Christ

One word to describe your mood

One thing that I am grateful for today

Prayer Request

R.E.S.T

A Reflective Path For Spiritual Growth

Receive The Word

Write out the scripture.

_____

_____

_____

_____

_____

Examine It's Truth

What is the scripture saying to you?

_____

_____

_____

_____

_____

Surrender

How can you apply this to your life?

_____

_____

_____

_____

_____

Talk To The Father

Ask God to help apply the verse.

_____

_____

_____

_____

_____

Meditation

Turn on soft music and close your eyes for 3-5 minutes

Inhale: Lord you breathe in me
Exhale: I am formed by your design

What can you do today to strengthen your walk with Christ

One word to describe your mood

One thing that I am grateful for today

Prayer Request

R.E.S.T
A Reflective Path For Spiritual Growth

Receive The Word

Write out the scripture.

_____
_____
_____
_____
_____

Examine It's Truth

What is the scripture saying to you?

_____
_____
_____
_____
_____

Surrender

How can you apply this to your life?

_____
_____
_____
_____
_____

Talk To The Father

Ask God to help apply the verse.

_____
_____
_____
_____
_____

MEDITATION

Turn on soft music and close your eyes for 3-5 minutes

Inhale: Lord you breathe in me
Exhale: I am formed by your design

What can you do today to strengthen your walk with Christ

One word to describe your mood

One thing that I am grateful for today

Prayer Request

R.E.S.T
A Reflective Path For Spiritual Growth

RECEIVE THE WORD

Write out the scripture.

_____

_____

_____

_____

_____

EXAMINE IT'S TRUTH

What is the scripture saying to you?

_____

_____

_____

_____

SURRENDER

How can you apply this to your life?

_____

_____

_____

_____

TALK TO THE FATHER

Ask God to help apply the verse.

_____

_____

_____

_____

MEDITATION

Turn on soft music and close your eyes for 3-5 minutes

Inhale: Lord you breathe in me
Exhale: I am formed by your design

What can you do today to strengthen your walk with Christ

One word to describe your mood

One thing that I am grateful for today

Prayer Request

R.E.S.T

A Reflective Path For Spiritual Growth

Receive The Word

Write out the scripture.
_____
_____
_____
_____
_____

Examine It's Truth

What is the scripture saying to you?
_____
_____
_____
_____
_____

Surrender

How can you apply this to your life?
_____
_____
_____
_____
_____

Talk To The Father

Ask God to help apply the verse.
_____
_____
_____
_____
_____

MEDITATION

Turn on soft music and close your eyes for 3-5 minutes

Inhale: Lord you breathe in me
Exhale: I am formed by your design

What can you do today to strengthen your walk with Christ

One word to describe your mood

One thing that I am grateful for today

Prayer Request

R.E.S.T

A Reflective Path For Spiritual Growth

RECEIVE THE WORD

Write out the scripture.

_____

_____

_____

_____

_____

EXAMINE IT'S TRUTH

What is the scripture saying to you?

_____

_____

_____

_____

SURRENDER

How can you apply this to your life?

_____

_____

_____

_____

TALK TO THE FATHER

Ask God to help apply the verse.

_____

_____

_____

_____

MEDITATION

Turn on soft music and close your eyes for 3-5 minutes

Inhale: Lord you breathe in me
Exhale: I am formed by your design

What can you do today to strengthen your walk with Christ

One word to describe your mood

One thing that I am grateful for today

Prayer Request

R.E.S.T
A Reflective Path For Spiritual Growth

Receive The Word

Write out the scripture.
_____
_____
_____
_____
_____

Examine It's Truth

What is the scripture saying to you?
_____
_____
_____
_____
_____

Surrender

How can you apply this to your life?
_____
_____
_____
_____
_____

Talk To The Father

Ask God to help apply the verse.
_____
_____
_____
_____
_____

MEDITATION

Turn on soft music and close your eyes for 3-5 minutes

Inhale: Lord you breathe in me
Exhale: I am formed by your design

What can you do today to strengthen your walk with Christ

One word to describe your mood

One thing that I am grateful for today

Prayer Request

R.E.S.T

A Reflective Path For Spiritual Growth

Receive The Word

Write out the scripture.

_____
_____
_____
_____
_____

Examine It's Truth

What is the scripture saying to you?

_____
_____
_____
_____
_____

Surrender

How can you apply this to your life?

_____
_____
_____
_____
_____

Talk To The Father

Ask God to help apply the verse.

_____
_____
_____
_____
_____

MEDITATION

Turn on soft music and close your eyes for 3-5 minutes

Inhale: Lord you breathe in me
Exhale: I am formed by your design

What can you do today to strengthen your walk with Christ

One word to describe your mood

One thing that I am grateful for today

Prayer Request

R.E.S.T
A Reflective Path For Spiritual Growth

Receive The Word

Write out the scripture.

_____
_____
_____
_____
_____

Examine It's Truth

What is the scripture saying to you?

_____
_____
_____
_____

Surrender

How can you apply this to your life?

_____
_____
_____
_____

Talk To The Father

Ask God to help apply the verse.

_____
_____
_____
_____

MEDITATION

Turn on soft music and close your eyes for 3-5 minutes

Inhale: Lord you breathe in me
Exhale: I am formed by your design

What can you do today to strengthen your walk with Christ

One word to describe your mood

One thing that I am grateful for today

Prayer Request

R.E.S.T
A Reflective Path For Spiritual Growth

Date:_____
S M T W T F S

Receive The Word

Write out the scripture.

_____
_____
_____
_____
_____

Examine It's Truth

What is the scripture saying to you?

_____
_____
_____
_____

Surrender

How can you apply this to your life?

_____
_____
_____
_____

Talk To The Father

Ask God to help apply the verse.

_____
_____
_____
_____

MEDITATION

Turn on soft music and close your eyes for 3-5 minutes

Inhale: Lord you breathe in me
Exhale: I am formed by your design

What can you do today to strengthen your walk with Christ

One word to describe your mood

One thing that I am grateful for today

Prayer Request

R.E.S.T
A Reflective Path For Spiritual Growth

Receive The Word

Write out the scripture.

_____
_____
_____
_____
_____
_____

Examine It's Truth

What is the scripture saying to you?

_____
_____
_____
_____
_____

Surrender

How can you apply this to your life?

_____
_____
_____
_____

Talk To The Father

Ask God to help apply the verse.

_____
_____
_____
_____

MEDITATION

Turn on soft music and close your eyes for 3-5 minutes

Inhale: Lord you breathe in me
Exhale: I am formed by your design

What can you do today to strengthen your walk with Christ

One word to describe your mood

One thing that I am grateful for today

Prayer Request

R.E.S.T
A Reflective Path For Spiritual Growth

RECEIVE THE WORD

Write out the scripture.

_____

_____

_____

_____

_____

EXAMINE IT'S TRUTH

What is the scripture saying to you?

_____

_____

_____

_____

SURRENDER

How can you apply this to your life?

_____

_____

_____

_____

TALK TO THE FATHER

Ask God to help apply the verse.

_____

_____

_____

_____

MEDITATION

Turn on soft music and close your eyes for 3-5 minutes

Inhale: Lord you breathe in me
Exhale: I am formed by your design

What can you do today to strengthen your walk with Christ

One word to describe your mood

One thing that I am grateful for today

Prayer Request

R.E.S.T
A Reflective Path For Spiritual Growth

Date:_____
S M T W T F S

Receive The Word

Write out the scripture.

_____

_____

_____

_____

_____

Examine It's Truth

What is the scripture saying to you?

_____

_____

_____

_____

Surrender

How can you apply this to your life?

_____

_____

_____

_____

Talk To The Father

Ask God to help apply the verse.

_____

_____

_____

_____

MEDITATION

Turn on soft music and close your eyes for 3-5 minutes

Inhale: Lord you breathe in me
Exhale: I am formed by your design

What can you do today to strengthen your walk with Christ

One word to describe your mood

One thing that I am grateful for today

Prayer Request

R.E.S.T

A Reflective Path For Spiritual Growth

Receive The Word

Write out the scripture.

_____

_____

_____

_____

_____

Examine It's Truth

What is the scripture saying to you?

_____

_____

_____

_____

_____

Surrender

How can you apply this to your life?

_____

_____

_____

_____

_____

Talk To The Father

Ask God to help apply the verse.

_____

_____

_____

_____

_____

MEDITATION

Turn on soft music and close your eyes for 3-5 minutes

Inhale: Lord you breathe in me
Exhale: I am formed by your design

What can you do today to strengthen your walk with Christ

One word to describe your mood

One thing that I am grateful for today

Prayer Request

R.E.S.T

A Reflective Path For Spiritual Growth

Receive The Word

Write out the scripture.

_____

_____

_____

_____

_____

Examine It's Truth

What is the scripture saying to you?

_____

_____

_____

_____

Surrender

How can you apply this to your life?

_____

_____

_____

_____

Talk To The Father

Ask God to help apply the verse.

_____

_____

_____

_____

MEDITATION

Turn on soft music and close your eyes for 3-5 minutes

Inhale: Lord you breathe in me
Exhale: I am formed by your design

What can you do today to strengthen your walk with Christ

One word to describe your mood

One thing that I am grateful for today

Prayer Request

Notes

Date

Notes

Date

Notes

Date

Notes

Date

Notes

Date

Notes

Date

Notes

Date

Notes

Date

Notes

Date

Notes

Date